The New International

Fondue

Cookbook

by Ed Callahan

edited and augmented by
Coleen and Robert Simmons

A Nitty Gritty® Cookbook

Printed in the U.S.A.

ISBN 1-55867-008-4

Cover photographer: Kathryn Opp
Food stylist: Carol Cooper Ladd
Cover art: Vicki L. Crampton

Table of Contents

Introduction

In the late 1960's and the 1970's, the serving of fondue seemed at the peak of popularity. Now, as the 1990's are born, there is a reawakening of interest in this delightful way of sharing food with family and friends. When we undertook the task of revising one of the earliest and most successful fondue books, we updated recipes and added many new recipes, including delicious hot dips and wonderful Oriental broths. We invite the reader to expand on these ideas, experimenting with different herbs and spices, different dippers, and even new opportunities for serving the many varieties of fondue.

Different types of fondue. From the original cheese fondue evolved the cooking of meats and seafood in hot oil (Fondue Bourguignonne), with all of its variations, and from America came dessert fondues. Although baked fondue, which also originated in this country, isn't at all similar to either the classic Swiss Fondue or Fondue Bourguignonne, it is a popular make-ahead party dish and it is included in this collection of fondues. Rarebits, on the other hand, bear no similarity of name but are quite like many of the cheese fondues. The major difference between a fondue and a rarebit seems to be whether the bread goes into or under the sauce. Rarebits can certainly be served with bread cubes for dipping as well as spooned over toast in the traditional manner.

Equipment. The classic-type cheese fondues can be prepared in an earthenware pot called a caquelon, or a metal pot over a heat source, or a chafing dish, or in a dish in a microwave oven (see *Classic Fondue in a Microwave,* page 7). Some fondue mixtures and rarebits do not stand up well over direct heat, and so they must be prepared and served over hot water. Because a chafing dish can be used in much the same way as a double boiler, it is by far the best to use under these circumstances. The various pots come in different sizes, shapes and prices. Special fondue forks are not essential but make the dipping process easier and more fun. It really isn't necessary to have special fondue equipment, but inexpensive sets are available and the more decorative the pot and other elements, the more festive the effect.

Entertain with fondue. Fondue is an excellent appetizer when you have friends in for cocktails. It's perfect when you're camping or on a trip to a ski or beach cabin. Retire to the living room after dinner with dessert fondue and steaming cups of hot coffee or tea. Or make fondue the main event for a meal or party. You may serve what you wish as long as the basic ingredients — good friends and a communal pot — are there.

Cheese Fondues and Hot Dips

Fondue doesn't have to be the classic Swiss variety to be delicious, and we've included interesting varieties of cheese fondues as well as several tasty hot dips. For today's busy cook, we've added recipes conveniently prepared in the microwave, but any cheese fondue recipe can be adapted to microwave cooking.

For cheese fondues, the best breads are hearty French, Italian or sourdough, cut so that each cube has some crust. But it is not necessary to restrict yourself to bread cubes. Bread sticks, crackers, toasted triangles of corn or flour tortillas, toasted pieces of pita bread or slices of cooked new potatoes are good for dipping. Celery and other raw vegetables are delicious with cheese fondue. Fruit and cheese have always complemented each other. Pieces of apple are perfect for cheddar fondues. Use your imagination and create a platter full of assorted "dippers."

Classic Fondue

How you eat is as much fun as what you eat! There are various Swiss traditions surrounding the unfortunate person who drops his bread in the fondue pot. A lady must pay her debt by kissing the man nearest her and a man pays by buying the wine; or perhaps it might mean only a loss of one's next turn.

½ lb. Emmenthaler cheese
½ lb. Gruyére cheese
1 clove garlic
2 cups dry white wine

1 tbs. lemon juice
2 tbs. flour
3 tbs. kirsch
dash nutmeg and paprika

Finely dice or coarsely shred cheese. It will melt better than if finely grated. Cut garlic clove in half. Rub fondue pot or saucepan and wooden spoon with cut side of garlic clove and then discard. Pour wine into pot and set over moderate heat. When hot (never boil), add lemon juice. Lightly toss flour with cheese. Drop by handfuls into hot wine. Stir constantly with wooden spoon. Allow each addition to melt before adding the next. Continue stirring in a figure eight motion until cheese is melted. Add kirsch and spices and serve.

Place the fondue pot in the middle of the table over low heat. Provide each guest (not more than 4 or 5 to a pot) with a fondue fork or bamboo skewer and bread cubes to dip into the cheese mixture.

The brown crust which remains in the bottom of the pot should be removed with a knife and divided among the diners. Many people think the crust is the best part of the fondue!

If serving fondue as a main course, the rest of the menu might consist of a crisp green salad tossed with raw vegetables and a light oil and fresh lemon juice dressing, chilled fruity white wine (dry Riesling or dry Chenin Blanc are particularly good choices), and for dessert a fresh fruit tray, baked apples or shortcakes topped with fresh or poached fruit.

Variations

Fondue Vermouth. Use dry vermouth instead of dry white wine.

Fondue Gorgonzola et Tilsiter. Use 1/3 Gorgonzola, 1/3 Tilsiter and 1/3 Gruyére cheeses.

Classic Fondue in a Microwave

Servings: 2-3

If you don't have a fondue pot, or if you are going to put the cooked fondue over a candle or other warmer that isn't hot enough to cook over, make it in the microwave in a soufflé dish, and then transfer the hot fondue to your fondue serving container. If you are using a microwavable dish, the fondue can be reheated uncovered for 1 to 2 minutes on high and returned to the serving table.

¼ lb. Emmenthaler cheese, coarsely grated
¼ lb. Gruyére cheese, coarsely grated
1 tbs. flour

1 cup dry white wine
1 clove garlic, cut in half
2 tsp. lemon juice
1 tbs. kirsch
dash nutmeg and paprika

Combine grated cheeses with flour and set aside. Place wine, garlic and lemon juice in a 1-quart soufflé dish or microwavable container and microwave uncovered on high for 2 to 3 minutes until boiling. Remove garlic and discard. Stir in grated cheese and flour mixture. Cook uncovered on medium power about 4 minutes until cheese is melted. Stir every 2 minutes. Stir in kirsch when mixture is almost melted and continue to cook until fondue is smooth. Sprinkle top of fondue with grated nutmeg and a dash of paprika. Transfer to a fondue pot for serving, or place a soufflé dish over a candle warmer on the table.

Pizza Fondue

Serve this fondue at a winter holiday gathering. Bread sticks make perfect dippers. Any left over makes a great lunch served over toasted English muffins.

½ medium onion, chopped
1 garlic clove, minced
¼ lb. ground beef
1 (10½ ozs.) jar pizza sauce
½ tsp. fennel seed
½ tsp. oregano
1 cup shredded cheddar cheese
½ cup shredded mozzarella cheese
bread sticks

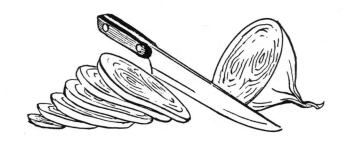

Brown onion, garlic and ground beef in a saucepan. Drain all excess liquid and fat. Return saucepan to medium heat, add pizza sauce and herbs; stir. Add cheese and stir until smooth. Transfer to a fondue pot for serving.

Continental Fondue

Servings: 4

Choose a lively young Soave or Pinot Grigio Italian white wine to accompany this dish. An antipasto tray of fresh vegetables, olives and thin sliced salami or other Italian deli meat is great with this.

1 clove garlic, cut in half
½ lb. Swiss cheese, minced
½ lb. Bel Paese or fontina cheese, minced
¾ cup dry white wine
2 tbs. brandy
French or Italian bread, cubed, or breadsticks

Rub bottom and sides of a fondue pot, saucepan or microwave dish with cut garlic. Add cheese and pour wine over it. Let stand at room temperature 4 to 5 hours. A few minutes before serving time, place over low heat, or microwave on medium. Stir frequently until cheese melts and mixture is smooth. Blend in brandy. Serve with bread cubes.

Fondue Sonoma

The dry Riesling gives this fondue a distinctive taste.

1 clove garlic, cut in half
2 cups California dry Riesling wine
1 lb. Swiss cheese, diced
1 tsp. flour
freshly ground pepper to taste
pinch grated nutmeg
2 tbs. California brandy
French or Italian bread, cubed

Rub the inside of a fondue pot or saucepan and wooden spoon with cut garlic. Pour in wine and warm over low heat. Toss cheese with flour. Add to heated wine, a little at a time. Stir until melted. Blend in seasoning and brandy. Serve with bread cubes.

Fondue Chablis for Two

Have a romantic supper in front of the fire with fondue, salad and a glass of wine.

½ lb. Swiss cheese, diced
½ tbs. flour
1 clove garlic, cut in half
½ cup California Chablis wine
dash nutmeg and pepper
French or Italian bread, cubed

   Toss cheese with flour. Rub fondue pot and wooden spoon with cut garlic. Pour in wine. Heat, but do not boil. Add cheese and stir until melted. Add seasonings, blend well and serve with bread cubes.

Pesto Fondue

Servings: 3-4

The zesty flavors of sweet basil and garlic spice up this dish.

Pesto

1 cup fresh basil leaves (approx. 1
 bunch), well packed
2 cloves garlic

1 tbs. full-flavored olive oil
2 tbs. grated Parmesan cheese
freshly ground pepper to taste

Process all ingredients in a food processor or blender until fairly smooth.

Fondue

¼ lb. fontina cheese, coarsely grated
¼ lb. Swiss or Gruyére cheese,
 coarsely grated

1 tbs. flour
1 cup white wine
1 tsp. lemon juice

Combine grated cheese with flour. Bring wine and lemon juice to a boil in a fondue pot or microwave dish, stir in cheese and cook over low heat until cheese melts. Stir in pesto and heat for another minute. Serve hot with bread sticks, bread cubes or small cooked new potatoes.

Spicy Bean Dip

This simple hot dip is a favorite for summer pool parties or after skiing. The little pockets of hot pepper cheese give it some zing.

1 (15 ozs.) can chili beans in sauce
½ tsp. ground cumin
2 ozs. hot pepper cheese, cut into very small dice

chopped fresh cilantro for garnish
tortilla chips and crisp vegetable slices for dipping

Drain chili beans, reserving 2 to 3 tbs. liquid. Place beans and cumin in a food processor bowl and process until smooth. Pour into a shallow microwave or soufflé dish. Stir in diced cheese. If using the microwave, heat uncovered on medium power 2 to 3 minutes, stir and continue to cook until beans are hot but cheese is not completely melted. Or heat in a small saucepan on the stove and pour into a warmed shallow serving container. Sprinkle with chopped cilantro. Serve warm.

Variation
Top hot dip with peeled, seeded, chopped fresh tomato pieces.

Egg Fondue

Servings: 4

This classic rich creamy fondue needs only a crisp salad and a glass of chardonnay to complete the meal.

1 clove garlic
¾ cup dry white wine
2 cups Swiss cheese, grated
2 tbs. butter
6 eggs, beaten
salt and freshly ground pepper to taste
French or Italian bread, cubed

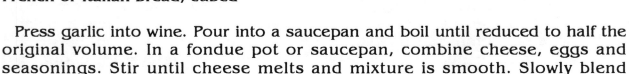

Press garlic into wine. Pour into a saucepan and boil until reduced to half the original volume. In a fondue pot or saucepan, combine cheese, eggs and seasonings. Stir until cheese melts and mixture is smooth. Slowly blend reduced wine into cheese mixture and serve with bread cubes.

Fondue de Berne

Dip small cooked new potatoes in addition to bread cubes for a delicious variation.

1 clove garlic, cut in half
½ cup dry white wine
I lb. Emmenthaler cheese, diced
4 egg yolks
⅓ cup cream
dash nutmeg and paprika
French or Italian bread, cubed

Rub the inside of a fondue pot with cut garlic. Pour in wine and heat over low heat. Add cheese gradually, stirring constantly until melted. Combine egg yolks, cream and seasonings. Slowly blend into cheese mixture. Cook, stirring, until mixture is thickened and creamy. Serve with bread cubes.

Creamy Clam Dip

Servings: 4-6

Here is a savory hot dip made with light cream cheese so you can indulge a little.

6 ozs. light cream cheese (Neufchâtel)
1 (6 ozs.) can chopped clams, drained, reserve juice
2-3 green onions, thinly sliced
2-3 oil-packed sun-dried tomatoes, diced

dash red pepper flakes
1/8 tsp. dried thyme
1/4 tsp. dry mustard
1 tbs. fresh parsley, chopped
1 small tomato, peeled, seeded, chopped for garnish

In a microwave, heat cream cheese on defrost 1 to 2 minutes to soften. Stir in drained clams, green onions, sun-dried tomatoes, red pepper flakes, thyme and mustard. Heat uncovered on medium for 2 minutes. Stir, add 1 to 2 tbs. reserved clam juice if mixture seems too thick, and heat for another minute. Top with parsley and fresh tomato pieces. Serve with crackers, crisp vegetable slices or tortilla chips.

Conventional Method

Combine all ingredients except for parsley and fresh tomato pieces, spoon into a shallow oven dish and bake at 350°F for 10 to 15 minutes until hot. Top with parsley and tomato pieces.

Fondue Jeune Fille

One or two marinated vegetable salads such as grated carrots or celery root can be done ahead and are a delicious accompaniment for this fondue. Serve with a dry Chenin Blanc.

¼ cup butter
2 tbs. flour
1½ cups dry white wine, heated
1 cup grated Swiss cheese
3 egg yolks
3 tbs. cream
nutmeg, salt and cayenne to taste
French or Italian bread, cubed

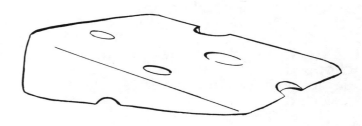

Melt butter in a fondue pot over moderate heat. Stir in flour and let bubble. Remove from heat. Slowly blend in wine. Return to heat and cook, stirring, until mixture is thickened. Add cheese. Combine egg yolks and cream. Carefully stir egg yolks into hot mixture until well blended. Season to taste and serve with bread cubes.

Chile Con Queso

Servings: 10-12

Need a snack for the football crowd, or something to go with Margaritas? This is the ticket. If there is any left, reheat and serve on English muffins for brunch.

1 tbs. vegetable oil
½ cup finely chopped onion
1 clove garlic, minced
1 tbs. flour
1 (4 ozs.) can green chilies, drained, chopped
1 large fresh tomato, peeled, seeded, chopped

1 tbs. hot taco sauce
¼ cup evaporated milk
6 ozs. Monterey Jack cheese, coarsely grated
6 ozs. sharp cheddar cheese, coarsely grated
tortilla chips or crisp vegetable slices for dipping

Place vegetable oil, onion and garlic in a microwavable container. Cook on high, uncovered, 1 to 2 minutes. Stir and continue to cook 1 to 2 minutes. Add cheese, stir and cook on medium power for 2 to 3 minutes. Stir and cook for 1 to 2 more minutes until cheese is melted. Pour into a fondue pot or serving dish. Serve warm.

Fonduta

This fondue is inspired by the Piedmont region of Italy, which is famous for fontina cheese.

¾ lb. fontina cheese, diced
¾ cup milk
2 tbs. butter
3 egg yolks
¼ tsp. white pepper
buttered toast fingers or Italian bread sticks

Combine cheese and milk. Refrigerate for several hours to soften cheese. When ready to prepare, transfer to a heavy saucepan. Cook over low heat, stirring constantly, about 5 minutes or until cheese melts. It may be somewhat stringy at this point. Beat yolks lightly and gradually stir about ¼ cup of hot cheese mixture into yolks. Pour slowly back into cheese mixture, beating constantly. Continue cooking over low heat until mixture becomes smooth and finally thickens. Serve with toast fingers or bread sticks.

Fondue with Chives

Chives give this fondue a pretty green hue and a subtle flavor. Serve as an appetizer in the living room with drinks before dinner.

3 tbs. butter
3½ tbs. finely chopped chives
1 cup dry white wine
½ lb. Swiss cheese, diced
1 tbs. flour
2 egg yolks, beaten
salt, dash Tabasco and nutmeg to taste
French or Italian bread, cubed

Melt butter in a fondue pot over low heat. Lightly sauté chives. Pour in wine and heat. Toss cheese with flour. Add to wine and stir until melted. Stir 3 tbs. hot cheese mixture into egg yolks. Slowly pour egg yolk mixture back into fondue pot, stirring constantly. Season and serve with bread cubes.

Creamy Spinach Dip

Servings: 6-8

This attractive green dip starts with frozen creamed spinach. Great with whole wheat toast fingers, cooked new potatoes or fresh mushrooms for dippers. Add some crumbled bacon or diced ham for a new twist.

1 (9 ozs.) pkg. frozen creamed spinach
1 tsp. butter
2-3 green onions, finely chopped
1 clove garlic, minced
⅓ cup evaporated milk

½ tsp. dry mustard
1 tsp. dill weed
1 tsp. Worcestershire sauce
2 ozs. Gruyére cheese, grated
3 tbs. Parmesan cheese, grated

Defrost spinach in a microwave according to package directions or defrost unopened pouch in boiling water for 12 minutes. In a soufflé dish put butter, green onions and garlic. Microwave uncovered for 1 to 2 minutes. Add defrosted spinach, evaporated milk and remaining ingredients. Stir well. Microwave on medium power 1 to 2 minutes, stir, and continue to cook another 1 to 2 minutes until cheese is melted.

Simple Simon Fondue

Servings: 4

Serve a light fruity Napa gamay or Italian Bardolino with this dish. Blanched broccoli or cauliflowerettes make terrific dippers, too.

1 garlic clove, cut in half
1 lb. mild cheddar or American cheese, diced
½ cup milk
1 tsp. dry mustard
salt, cayenne and paprika to taste
1 egg yolk, beaten
1 egg white, beaten to stiff peaks
French or Italian bread, cubed

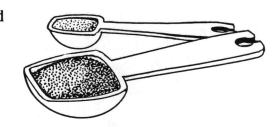

Rub a fondue pot with cut garlic. Add cheese. Place pot over low heat and stir cheese until melted. Combine milk, seasonings and beaten egg yolk. Slowly blend into hot melted cheese. Cook until thickened. Carefully fold in stiffly beaten egg white and serve immediately with bread cubes.

Cheddar Cheese Fondue

Servings: 4

The mustard complements the cheddar cheese and gives this fondue a little character. Use whole wheat or rye bread for dippers and serve with a full-bodied ale.

1 tsp. dry mustard
3 tbs. butter
3 tbs. flour
freshly ground pepper to taste
1 cup milk
2 cups diced cheddar cheese,
French or Italian bread cubes

Melt butter in a saucepan over medium heat. Add flour, mustard and pepper; cook 1 minute. Remove from heat. Slowly stir in milk; return to heat and cook, stirring, until mixture boils. Add cheese and stir until melted. Transfer to a fondue pot and serve with bread cubes.

Cheddar Fondue with Horseradish

Servings: 4

Serve this bold-flavored fondue on the Superbowl party buffet or for a Friday night poker game.

½ lb. cheddar cheese, diced
1 tbs. butter
⅓ cup milk, warmed
1 tsp. Worcestershire sauce
¾ tsp. prepared horseradish
salt and freshly ground pepper to taste
1 egg yolk, beaten
1 egg white, beaten to stiff peaks
2 tbs. sherry
paprika

Melt cheese and butter in a fondue pot over low heat. Slowly stir in milk and seasonings. Blend in beaten egg yolk. Cook, stirring, for a few minutes until thickened and smooth. Remove from heat. Fold in stiffly beaten egg white and sherry. Dust with paprika. Serve with bread cubes.

Cider Fondue

Make this for your Little Leaguers, Girl Scouts or any group with a hearty appetite. Serve with the same nonalcoholic cider used in the fondue.

1 tsp. flour
1 tsp. dry mustard
2 cups apple cider
2 lbs. cheddar cheese, diced
2 tbs. butter
salt and freshly ground pepper to taste
French or Italian bread, cubed

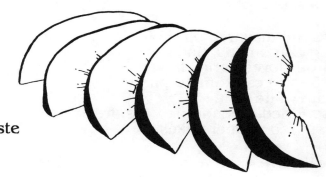

Mix flour and mustard together. Blend into ½ cup cider with a fork. Heat remaining cider in a saucepan over low heat. Add cheese and butter and stir constantly until smooth and cheese is melted. Add mustard mixture and seasonings. Pour into a fondue pot and serve with bread cubes.

Greek Shrimp Fondue

Servings: 4

The wonderful Mediterranean flavors make this fondue perfect for dipping cooked shrimp, scallops and small creamer potatoes. If there is any left, it makes a terrific pasta sauce, or pour it over grilled polenta squares.

2 tbs. full-flavored olive oil
4-5 green onions, finely chopped
2 large cloves garlic, finely chopped
1 (15 ozs.) can tomato puree
1/3 cup white wine
1 tsp. dried oregano or 1 tbs. fresh
1/8 tsp. red pepper flakes

5-6 ozs. feta cheese, crumbled
2 tbs. finely chopped parsley,
salt and freshly ground pepper
  to taste
1 lb. cooked medium shrimp or sea
  scallops, or combination
2-3 small cooked potatoes per person

Heat olive oil in a fondue pot. Add onion and garlic and sauté 1 to 2 minutes until onion softens. Add tomato puree, white wine, oregano and red pepper flakes; heat. Note: tomato sauces seem to splatter in a fondue pot, so watch carefully and keep just at a simmer. Add feta cheese and continue to cook until cheese has mostly melted. Add parsley, salt and pepper. Serve hot.

Hot Pepper Cheese Fondue

Servings: 4

This is a simple, zesty fondue that is great with tortilla chips, whole wheat toast fingers or crisp vegetables for dippers.

2 tbs. butter
2 tbs. flour
1½ cups milk
6 ozs. hot pepper cheese, coarsely grated
2 tbs. grated Parmesan cheese
¼ tsp. dry mustard

Melt butter in a fondue pot, add flour and cook 2 minutes. Slowly stir in milk and cook until mixture thickens. Add both cheeses and dry mustard. Cook until cheese melts and mixture is hot.

In a Microwave

Reduce milk to 1¼ cups and heat uncovered on high until milk is steaming. Combine flour with grated cheeses and stir into hot milk mixture with mustard. Cook on medium for 2 minutes, stir, and continue to cook another 1 to 2 minutes until cheeses are melted. Pour into a fondue pot or serving dish.

Fondue Marseillaise

Servings: 4

This light creamy fondue makes an excellent appetizer, or it makes a lovely luncheon when served with crusty French bread and a crisp green salad. Serve with a dry Chenin Blanc.

2 cups milk
1 cup grated Swiss cheese
3 tbs. flour
1 tbs. Worcestershire sauce
salt to taste
½ tsp. dry mustard
1 lb. small cooked shrimp

Blend all ingredients except shrimp in a blender or food processor until well combined. Pour into a saucepan or a microwave dish and cook over medium heat or on medium power in the microwave, stirring constantly, until smooth and thickened. Pour into a fondue pot and serve with shrimp "dippers."

Fondue Avec Oeufs

Servings: 4-6

This makes a substantial brunch or luncheon dish. Serve with Canadian bacon, toasted English muffins and a fresh fruit platter.

6 hard-cooked eggs
3/4 cup bread crumbs
3 tbs. finely chopped parsley
2 tbs. finely chopped chives

1/4 tsp. dill weed
salt, cayenne and paprika to taste
Fondue Chablis, page 11

Cut eggs in half lengthwise. Remove yolks and mash with bread crumbs and seasonings. Stuff egg whites with filling. Spoon heated fondue over eggs, dust with additional paprika and serve.

Hot Oil and Hot Broth Fondues

Hot oil fondue, traditionally called Fondue Bourguignonne, according to legend had its beginning centuries ago in the famous vineyards of the Burgundy region of France. During the harvest season, the grapes had to be picked at the precise time of ripeness; there was no time for the harvesters to eat. Someone had the idea of keeping a pot of fat boiling so each worker could quickly cook his own pieces of meat in spare moments. Whether or not the story is true, the Swiss have developed the idea to its present form and honored the Burgundy origin by naming the dish Fondue Bourguignonne.

The right equipment for meat fondue is extremely important. The pot must be made of metal which will tolerate high heat and keep the oil hot. It must set securely on its stand to avoid the danger of tipping. The traditional pot is wide at the base and narrow at the top to eliminate some of the spattering and retain the heat. A tray beneath the pot will help catch some of the spatters; many fondue sets come with a tray.

The heat source, over which the fondue pot sets, must be adequate enough to keep the oil hot during the entire cooking process. Those which can be adjusted are best; butane, alcohol or electric burners are preferable. Forks used for cooking should be a minimum of 10 inches in length with long tines for securing the food. Many have color-keyed handles or tips so each person can recognize his own. Special fondue plates with sections for the sauces are attractive, but sauces can be served in individual dishes as well.

Never have the pot more than half full of oil. And, unless your fondue pot is electric, it is better to heat the oil to the desired temperature on the range and then bring it to the table. The recommended temperature is about 375°F. Test with a deep fat thermometer or cubes of bread or meat. Bread will brown in about 60 seconds at that temperature and the oil will sizzle upon contact with the meat, which will start to brown immediately. Adjust the heat source to keep the oil as close to that temperature during cooking as possible. A good quality of oil should always be used. For extra flavor, half oil and half clarified butter are sometimes used. Be careful to keep the temperature below 400°F or the clarified butter will begin to smoke.

Hot broth recipes are also found in this section, and you will find them a delightful and healthy variation to use with your fondue pot.

For the best fondue, use good cuts of high quality meat or seafood. Remove all fat, cut into bite-sized pieces and pat dry to cut down on spattering. Take the meat from the refrigerator about 30 minutes before using. It will cook faster and it will help to maintain the temperature of the oil if the meat is not cold. Guests should be provided with dinner forks, since fondue forks become extremely hot and are not safe for eating.

We have included some wonderful broth fondues in this section as well, for a delicious, lower calorie change of pace.

Besides a variety of sauces, a crisp green salad, crusty French bread or rolls and glasses of wine are all that are needed to accompany any of these fondues. However, there are no set rules; serve any menu that pleases you.

Sauces

sic Fondue Bourguignonne

.ıs is the basic hot oil fondue from which the variations have developed.

2 lbs. beef filet or boneless sirloin
oil to fill ½ fondue pot
3-5 dipping sauces
salt and freshly ground pepper to taste

   Trim all fat from meat and cut into bite-sized pieces. Arrange on small plates so each guest may have his own. Heat oil in fondue pot to about 375°F. Place in the center of the table over a heat source. Pieces of meat should be speared on fondue forks and cooked to taste (about 30 seconds for medium-rare). Remove meat from fondue fork, season and dip into sauces as desired.

Mixed Grill Fondue

Servings: 4

Serve with creamy scalloped potatoes, a marinated vegetable salad and a Cabernet Sauvignon.

½ lb. beef filet or boneless sirloin
½ lb. lean pork
½ lb. veal cutlets, pounded
4 veal kidneys
4 chicken livers
oil to fill ½ fondue pot
salt and freshly ground pepper to taste

Trim all fat from meat and cut into bite-sized pieces. Arrange several pieces of each meat on a small plate for each guest. Heat oil in a fondue pot to about 375°F, maintain heat over heat source and allow each guest to cook meat to taste. Serve with seasonings and assorted sauces.

Poultry Fondue

Servings: 4

Either a full bodied Chardonnay or a Pinot Noir make perfect accompaniments. Make a spicy Oriental style noodle salad with slivered fresh vegetables to serve with this.

2 lbs. chicken or turkey breast meat
oil to fill ½ fondue pot
3-5 sauces for dipping
salt and freshly ground pepper to taste

Remove skin from breast meat and cut into bite-sized pieces. Arrange on plates for guests; heat oil in a fondue pot to 375°F and allow each guest to cook meat to taste. Serve with seasonings and assorted sauces.

Lamb Fondue

Servings: 4

Baked tomatoes stuffed with onion and thyme-scented rice, and a salad of crisp romaine leaves dressed with a light vinaigrette and sprinkled with Parmesan cheese would be perfect accompaniments. Serve with a fruity zinfandel.

2 lbs. tender lamb
oil to fill ½ fondue pot
3-5 sauces for dipping
salt and freshly ground pepper to taste

Ask your butcher for a tender cut. A small leg might be the best buy. Remove all fat from meat and cut into bite-sized pieces. Arrange on plates for guests; heat oil to 375°F and allow each guest to cook meat to taste. Serve with seasonings and assorted sauces.

Pork or Ham Fondue

Servings: 4

Try this with a white zinfandel. Cinnamon-flavored chunky applesauce and crisp potato wedges will round out this dinner.

2 lbs. lean pork or ham
oil to fill ½ fondue pot
3-5 sauces for dipping
salt and freshly ground pepper to taste

Cut meat into bite-sized pieces. Arrange on plates for guests; heat oil to 375°F and allow each guest to cook meat to taste. Serve with seasonings and assorted sauces.

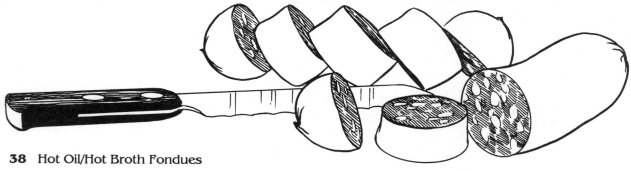

Tempura

Be sure seafood, chicken and vegetable pieces are dry and almost room temperature before dipping them into the batter. Then simply cook in hot oil until golden. Cauliflower, snow peas, sliced carrots, red or green bell pepper strips, green beans and thin asparagas are just a few of the vegetables that are delicious this way.

½ lb. seafood, cut into bite-sized pieces
½ lb. chicken or turkey, cut into bite-sized pieces
assorted vegetables, cut into bite-sized pieces

Batter

1 egg yolk, at room temperature
1 cup ice water
1 cup flour

pinch of salt
white pepper to taste
flour to coat dipping ingredients

Beat egg yolk with a fork, add cold water and mix well. Add flour and just stir to combine. Batter should be quite thin, about the consistency of cream. Add more ice water if necessary. Mixture should leave just a thin coating on seafood or vegetables when dipped. Blot prepared vegetables or seafood in a paper towel and then roll in flour. Dip into the tempura batter and cook immediately in hot oil. Serve with **Sweet and Sour Sauce** or **Teriyaki Sauce**.

Bagna Caôda

Bagna Caôda is a delicious Italian hot olive oil and garlic dip for fresh vegetables. The anchovies melt into the hot oil and add a zesty complex flavor to the dish. Even non-anchovy lovers have been known to enjoy this preparation. Vegetables for dipping can be prepared in advance, covered and refrigerated until you are ready to serve.

½ cup olive oil
½ cup butter
3 medium cloves garlic, finely chopped
1 (2 ozs.) can flat anchovy fillets,
  finely chopped, with oil

½ tsp. salt
⅛ tsp. red pepper flakes
vegetables and bread cubes for
  dipping

Combine olive oil and butter in a fondue pot or small saucepan. Heat oil until butter starts to melt. Add garlic, chopped anchovy fillets with their oil, salt and red pepper flakes. Heat gently over low heat for about 10 minutes, stirring occasionally, until garlic is soft and anchovies are dissolved. Serve warm with a colorful variety of vegetables, raw or cooked. The vegetables are speared on the fondue fork and the cube of bread in the left hand is used to catch the savory drips of oil from the vegetables.

Raw Vegetables for Dipping

Red, green and yellow pepper pieces, carrot slices or thin baby carrots, fennel or celery strips, zucchini or yellow summer squash slices, small mushroom caps, jicama slices, green onions, cucumber slices.

Cooked Vegetables for Dipping

Small creamer potatoes; snow peas, broccoli or cauliflower flowerettes, blanched for 1 minute in boiling water or microwaved briefly.

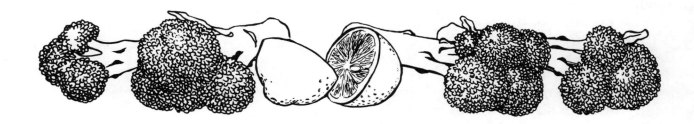

Seafood Fondue

Servings: 2-3

This dish can be served as a fondue, dipping each morsel of cooked seafood into a garlicky mayonnaise, or cook the seafood all at once in the broth, ladle over rice, and top with aioli, French style. Each person should have a small bowl of cooked rice to catch the drops of broth from the cooked seafood.

1 (14½ ozs.) can chicken broth
1 (8 ozs.) bottle clam juice
⅓ cup white wine
2 tbs. soy sauce
dash Tabasco
3-4 green onions, thinly sliced
1 thin slice fresh ginger
1 clove garlic, minced
½ cup carrots, finely diced
¼ lb. sea scallops, cut in half if large
¼ lb. medium sized shrimp, peeled, deveined
½ lb. ling cod, halibut, or salmon cut into bite-sized pieces
1 cup green peas or 5-6 slivered fresh snow peas

1 cup mushrooms, thinly sliced
3-4 cups hot cooked rice

Combine chicken broth, clam juice, white wine, soy sauce, Tabasco, green onions, ginger, garlic and carrot in a fondue pot or microwave dish. Bring to a boil. Arrange seafood pieces on a large platter. Each person should have a plate with a small rice bowl of hot rice, a spoonful of aioli and a fondue fork. Cook individual pieces of seafood in the hot broth 2 to 3 minutes until just cooked, dip in aioli and eat. When most of the seafood has been cooked, add the green peas and mushroom slices to the broth with the rest of the fish. Cook 2 to 3 minutes and spoon over rice in individual bowls. Stir in a spoonful of aioli.

Aioli
6-8 large cloves garlic
2 egg yolks
1½ tbs. lemon juice
1 tsp. Dijon mustard
dash cayenne or Tabasco sauce

½ cup full-flavored olive oil
¾ cup vegetable oil
salt and white pepper to taste
2-3 tsp. boiling water

Mince garlic in a food processor. Add egg yolks, lemon juice, cayenne and mustard; process for a few seconds. Slowly add olive and vegetable oils, processing until mixture thickens. Stir in 1 to 2 tsp. boiling water. The sauce should be thick and shiny. Add salt and white pepper to taste. If made ahead, refrigerate until just before serving.

Low Calorie Fondue

This version of fondue is very popular with calorie watchers. Meats and vegetables are cooked in a delicious broth instead of being deep-fried. Broth may be substituted for oil in any of the previous recipes. After the meat has all been cooked, the flavorful broth can be served alone or over cooked rice or noodles as a tasty bonus.

2½ cups beef or chicken broth
1¼ cups water
½ cup dry white wine
½ bunch green onions, chopped
1 stalk celery, chopped
sprigs of parsley
salt and freshly ground pepper to taste
1 tsp. fines herbes

Simmer ingredients in a saucepan for 10 minutes. Remove from heat and let stand 2 hours. Strain into a fondue pot and bring to a boil.

Beef Mizutaki

Servings: 4

Mizutaki is a term which simply means "boiling water." It is known sometimes as shabu-shabu. Ancient Mongolia gets credit for originating this simple, elegant dish. It is also a friendly dish, the whole meal being served from a common bowl. Plenty of hot rice should be available. This is one meal where the soup follows rather than precedes the main course. You will be making the soup as you cook the meat. A suitable implement for cooking mizutaki is one that will keep water bubbling-hot: chafing dish, electric frying pan or fondue pot.

3-4 cups beef broth (enough to fill ½ container)
1-1½ lbs. market or Spencer steak, sliced ⅛ thick
1 block tofu cut into bite-sized pieces
8-10 fresh shitaki mushrooms or 3-4 dried, softened in warm water
1 bunch fresh spinach leaves
1 bunch green onions, cut in 2" lengths
1 lb. Chinese cabbage, shredded in 2" lengths
hot cooked rice

Bring beef broth to a boil. Add tofu and cook just long enough to warm through. Add mushrooms, spinach, green onions and cabbage. Cook for 1 to 2 minutes until wilted, add meat and cook 1 to 2 minutes. Remove cooked ingredients with chopsticks to individual serving bowls and serve with rice and dipping sauces. After eating the meat and vegetables, spoon out some of the stock and drink as a broth, seasoning with salt, pepper or a few drops of dipping sauce.

Horseradish Dipping Sauce
½ cup dark soy sauce
1 tbs. wasabi horseradish, finely grated

Ginger Dipping Sauce
½ cup dark soy sauce
1 tbs. fresh ginger, finely grated

Citrus Dipping Sauce
½ cup soy sauce
¼ cup lemon juice
¼ cup orange juice

Chicken Mizutaki

Servings: 4

Bite-sized pieces of chicken also make a delicious mizutaki. Arrange chicken and vegetables in an attractive pattern on a platter. Chopsticks work well to put the individual morsels into the bubbling hot broth.

3-4 cups chicken broth
1-1½ boneless chicken breasts,
  cut in bite-sized pieces
1 block tofu, cut in bite-sized pieces
4-6 medium dried shiitake mushrooms,
  softened in warm water

4-6 fresh mushrooms, thinly sliced
2 carrots, cut in ¼" diagonal slices
1 bunch green onions, cut in 2" lengths
1 lb. Chinese cabbage, cut in 1"
  squares
hot cooked rice

Bring broth to a boil, add chicken and cook until tender, about 10 minutes. Add tofu and just heat through. Cook mushrooms, carrots, green onions and cabbage until wilted, 2 to 3 minutes. Remove cooked meat and vegetables to serving bowls. Serve with rice and dipping sauce. Spoon out some of the broth and drink after eating the meat and vegetables, seasoning with salt or dipping sauce. See **Beef Mizutaki**, page 46.

Anchovy Sauce

If you love the distinctive flavor of anchovies, this sauce is for you.

1 cup mayonnaise
1 tbs. chopped parsley
1 tbs. capers, drained
1 tbs. chopped anchovies

1 hard-cooked egg, finely chopped
1 tsp. dry mustard
garlic powder to taste

Combine ingredients. Chill until serving.

Avocado Sauce

1½ cups

This sauce adds a "south-of-the-border" flavor.

2 ripe avocados
2 tbs. minced onion
1 tbs. lemon juice

1 tbs. mayonnaise
2 drops Tabasco sauce
salt to taste

Mash avocados. Stir in onion, lemon juice, mayonnaise, Tabasco and salt. Mix until well blended.

Easy Barbecue Sauce

1½ cups

This is especially good with chicken.

1 (12 ozs.) bottle hot catsup
3 tbs. vinegar

2 tsp. celery seed
1 garlic clove, cut in half

Combine ingredients. Chill several hours. Remove garlic before serving. May also be served warm, if desired.

Spicy Catsup

¾ cup

This is delicious with seafood. Use any left over for cocktail sauce.

¾ cup catsup
2 tbs. vinegar

½ tsp. prepared horseradish

Combine ingredients. Chill.

Island Peanut Sauce

2/3 cup

Use this spicy Indonesian dipping sauce for chicken, pork or beef.

½ cup chicken stock
¼ cup peanut butter
¼ tsp. finely minced garlic
¼ tsp. finely grated fresh ginger
2 green onions, white part only,

finely minced
2 tsp. brown sugar
2 tsp. dark soy sauce
1 tsp. cider vinegar
dash Tabasco sauce

Combine all ingredients in a small saucepan. Heat on low, stirring constantly, until mixture boils. Add a little more chicken stock or water if mixture is not thin enough for dipping. This sauce can be made ahead and reheated in a microwave on medium power when ready to serve.

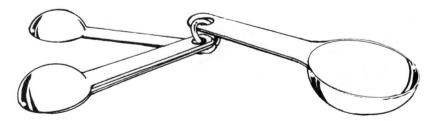

Sour Cream Horseradish Sauce

1¼ cups

This classic creamy sauce goes well with everything.

1 cup (½ pt.) sour cream
3 tbs. prepared horseradish, well
   drained

1 tsp. lemon juice or vinegar
salt to taste
dash paprika

Combine all ingredients. Chill.

Sour Cream Mustard Sauce

1¼ cups

Use a Dijon-style mustard.

1 cup (½ pt.) sour cream
3 tbs. prepared mustard
2 tbs. chopped green onion

salt and freshly ground pepper to
   taste

Combine ingredients. Chill.

Curry Mayonnaise

1 cup

Here is a dipping sauce with the flavor of India.

½ cup mayonnaise
½ cup sour cream

1 tsp. lemon juice
1 tsp. curry powder

Combine mayonnaise and sour cream. Blend in lemon juice and curry. Taste. Add more seasoning if desired. Chill.

Roquefort Butter

1 cup

A French classic, this is wonderful with beef.

4 ozs. Roquefort cheese
½ cup butter
1 tbs. prepared mustard

1 clove garlic, crushed
1 tsp. Worcestershire sauce

Blend ingredients together well. Serve at room temperature.

Sour Cream Chutney Sauce

1 cup

Use this sauce with chicken.

¾ cup sour cream
¼ cup chutney

pinch curry powder

Combine ingredients and chill to blend flavors.

Blender Béarnaise Sauce

1 cup

The blender makes this classic sauce foolproof.

4 shallots
½ cup tarragon vinegar
2 egg yolks

salt and cayenne pepper to taste
1 tsp. *each* parsley, chives, tarragon
½ cup butter, melted, cooled

Place shallots and vinegar in a blender container and run at low speed 15 seconds or until shallots are chopped. Pour mixture into a small saucepan and boil until liquid is reduced to 2 tablespoons. Strain; pour liquid back into blender container. Add egg yolks, salt, cayenne, parsley, chives and tarragon. Blend on lowest speed. Gradually pour in cooled butter and stop blending when sauce thickens.

Piquant Sauce for Ham

2/3 cup

The perfect sauce with ham. Try it with pork chunks, too.

1/2 cup currant jelly
2 tbs. prepared mustard

1 1/2 tsp. lemon juice
1/8 tsp. cinnamon

Combine in a saucepan. Heat until jelly melts.

Teriyaki Sauce

3/4 cup

The flavor of Japan is delicious with fish or meat.

1/2 cup soy sauce
1 clove garlic, minced
1 tbs. brown sugar

1 tsp. fresh ginger, grated
1/4 cup sake or dry sherry

Combine ingredients.

Tangy Mint Sauce for Lamb

¾ cup

Mint and lamb are a classic English combination.

½ cup mint jelly
2 tbs. butter
2 tbs. cider vinegar

1 tbs. lemon juice
½ tsp. dry mustard

Combine ingredients in a small saucepan. Stir over low heat until jelly melts and mixture comes to a boil.

Tartar Sauce

1¼ cups

Your favorite fish sauce is easy to prepare at home.

½ cup mayonnaise
½ cup sour cream
1 tbs. chopped stuffed green olives

1 tbs. minced parsley
1 tbs. chopped capers
1 tbs. chopped sweet pickles

Combine mayonnaise and sour cream. Fold in remaining ingredients. Chill to blend flavors.

Sweet and Sour Sauce

1 cup

These Chinese flavors are delicious with chicken, fish, ham and pork, but not beef.

½ cup orange juice
½ cup cider vinegar
½ cup sugar
2 tbs. tomato paste
½ tsp. sesame oil
2-3 drops Tabasco
1 tbs. cornstarch dissolved in
   2 tbs. water

Combine all ingredients except cornstarch in a small saucepan or microwave dish. Bring to a boil. Stir in 1 tbs. of dissolved cornstarch mixture and continue to cook for 1 to 2 minutes. Add more cornstarch if a thicker sauce is desired.

Baked Fondues

Although baked fondues are not as spectacular as soufflés, they do have a similar texture and are sometimes thought of as simplified soufflés. Happily the fear of having a beautiful soufflé collapse on its way to the table doesn't exist with its country cousin, which originated many years ago as a practical way of using stale bread or bread crumbs. Many variations of this nutritious and economical discovery have appeared over the years, sometimes called "strata," and they still are a favorite make-ahead dish. Baked fondues with meat or fish are perfect for main courses and lend themselves beautifully to buffet brunches or suppers.

A buffet supper might consist of a baked main dish fondue, your favorite tossed salad, a pretty molded salad, buttered vegetable, crusty rolls, a light fruit dessert and a beverage, most of which can easily be prepared in advance.

Easy Baked Cheese Fondue

Servings: 2

Use any full-flavored cheese for this dish—Swiss, cheddar, blue-veined or a combination.

1 cup fresh bread crumbs
1 cup milk, warmed
1 cup (4 ozs.) grated cheese
2 tbs. butter, melted
salt and cayenne pepper to taste
1 egg yolk, slightly beaten
1 egg white, beaten to stiff peaks
Parmesan cheese for topping

Soak bread crumbs in milk. Stir in cheese, butter, salt and cayenne. Add beaten egg yolk. Fold in stiffly beaten egg white. Pour mixture into a well-buttered casserole. Sprinkle with Parmesan cheese. Bake at 375°F for 1 hour or until a knife inserted in the center comes out clean.

Baked Cheddar Cheese Fondue

Make this the night before for an easy, satisfying company breakfast or brunch.

8 slices bread, buttered
1¾ lbs. sharp cheddar, grated
6 eggs
2½ cups half and half
1 tbs. minced onion
1 tsp. brown sugar
½ tsp. Beau Monde seasoning
½ tsp. Worcestershire sauce
½ tsp. dry mustard
salt and freshly ground pepper to taste

Dice bread. Scatter half of bread cubes on the bottom of a buttered casserole. Add half of the cheese, then another layer of bread and top with remaining cheese. Beat eggs. Blend with remaining ingredients and pour over cheese. Refrigerate for 1 hour. Bake in a 300°F oven for 1 hour or until a knife inserted in the center comes out clean.

Baked Fondue Maria

Servings: 2-3

To give this fondue extra zip, use some hot pepper cheese; or add ½ cup sautéed onions or a small can of crumbled onion rings before folding in the egg yolks.

1 clove garlic, cut in half
1 cup milk, warmed
1 cup fresh bread crumbs
1 cup (4 ozs.) diced cheese
1 tbs. butter
salt, cayenne and paprika to taste
3 egg yolks, beaten
3 egg whites, beaten to stiff peaks

Rub bottom and sides of a casserole dish with cut garlic and then butter it well. Combine milk, crumbs, cheese, butter and seasonings in a heavy saucepan. Cook over medium heat until cheese melts and mixture is smooth. Remove from heat. Stir in beaten egg yolks. Fold in stiffly beaten egg whites and pour into prepared casserole. Bake in a 350°F oven 35-40 minutes, or until a knife inserted in the center comes out clean.

Petite Baked Fondues

Almost any cheese you may have on hand will work in this recipe. For added flavor fold in ½ cup finely diced ham or some crumbled bacon bits.

1 cup fresh bread crumbs
2 cups milk
2 eggs beaten
½ lb. cheese, grated
1 tbs. butter, melted
1 tsp. Dijon mustard
1 tsp. dried Italian herbs
dash Tabasco sauce
salt and freshly ground pepper to taste
¼ cup grated Parmesan cheese

Combine bread crumbs and milk. Add eggs, cheese, melted butter and seasonings. Pour into buttered individual ramekins or a casserole. Sprinkle with Parmesan cheese. Bake in a 300°F oven for 1 hour, or until a knife inserted in the center comes out clean.

Baked Tuna Fondue

Servings: 2-3

This is a quick dish to put together for a weekday dinner. Serve it with coleslaw or a grated carrot salad. You can relax while it bakes.

1 cup fresh bread crumbs
1 cup milk, warmed
1 (6½ ozs.) can tuna, drained
3 tbs. diced pimiento
1 cup (4 ozs.) grated cheese
2 tbs. butter, melted
salt and cayenne pepper to taste
2 egg yolks
2 egg whites
Parmesan cheese for topping

Soak bread crumbs in milk. Add tuna, pimiento, cheese, butter, salt and cayenne. Beat egg yolks until creamy. Stir into cheese mixture. Fold in stiffly beaten egg whites. Pour into a well-buttered casserole. Top with Parmesan cheese. Bake in a 325°F oven 35 to 45 minutes, or until a knife inserted in the center comes out clean.

Baked Fondue with Beer

Slip a slice of ham or thin Canadian bacon into these sandwiches for a heartier dish.

8 slices bread, buttered
8 slices American cheese
3 eggs, beaten
1 tsp. Worcestershire sauce
½ tsp. dry mustard
1 cup beer

Make 4 sandwiches using buttered bread and four slices of cheese. Place in a square buttered baking dish and top with remaining cheese slices. Beat eggs and seasonings together. Stir in beer and pour over sandwiches. Bake in a 350°F oven about 40 minutes, or until set.

Baked Cheddar Beer Fondue

This is a great dish for a blustery cold evening or after skiing. Serve with beer, of course.

1 cup milk
2 tbs. chopped onion
1 cup beer
3 cups (12 ozs.) grated cheddar cheese
2½ cups bread cubes
salt to taste

½ tsp. dry mustard
4 egg yolks, beaten
4 egg whites, beaten to stiff peaks
2 tbs. butter
2 tsp. caraway seeds

Combine milk and onion in a saucepan. Scald over low heat. Add beer, cheese, 2 cups bread cubes, salt and dry mustard. Stir until cheese melts. Lightly beat egg yolks. Slowly add to mixture, stirring constantly. Fold in stiffly beaten egg whites and pour into a well-buttered casserole. Dot with butter; sprinkle with caraway seeds and remaining ½ cup bread cubes. Bake in a 325°F oven 1¼ hours, or until a knife inserted in the center comes out clean.

Baked Parisian Fondue

Servings: 8

This dish will star at a weekend brunch. Start with Bloody Marys or champagne and orange juice. Serve with a platter of fresh fruit.

1½ loaves French bread, sliced
½ cup soft butter
½ cup prepared mustard
1½ lbs. cheddar cheese, sliced
4 eggs, beaten
5 cups milk, heated
1½ tsp. Worcestershire sauce
salt, cayenne and paprika to taste

Spread bread slices with butter and mustard. Cover bottom of large, well-buttered casserole with slices of bread. Cover bread with cheese slices. Continue until bread and cheese are all used, ending with bread. Combine eggs, hot milk, Worcestershire sauce and seasonings. Pour over bread. Refrigerate several hours or overnight. Bake in a 350°F oven 1½ hours, or until a knife inserted in the center comes out clean.

Baked Crab Meat Fondue

Servings: 4

This recipe is equally good with cooked salad shrimp instead of crab. Serve with a Sauvignon Blanc or Chardonnay for a company supper.

2 cups milk
¼ cup butter
1¾ cups bread crumbs
1 clove garlic, minced
½ tsp. minced onion
salt and freshly ground pepper to taste
¼ tsp. ground ginger
5 eggs, separated
1 cup (4 ozs.) grated Monterey Jack cheese
6-8 ozs. fresh or imitation crab meat, flaked

Heat milk in a saucepan. Add butter, bread crumbs, garlic, minced onion, salt, pepper and ginger. Add beaten egg yolks. Cook over low heat, stirring constantly until thickened. Stir in cheese and crab meat. Fold in stiffly beaten egg whites and pour into a well-buttered casserole. Bake in a 325°F oven 1½ hours, or until a knife inserted in the center comes out clean.

Baked La Fondue Hestere

Here is a new twist to tuna sandwiches, hot and savory.

1 (6½ ozs.) can tuna, drained
1 cup finely chopped celery
2-3 green onions, finely sliced
¼ cup mayonnaise
1 tbs. dry mustard
½ tsp. salt
12 slices bread
6 slices cheddar cheese
3 eggs, beaten
2½ cups milk
2 tsp. Worcestershire sauce

   Combine tuna, celery, onions, mayonnaise, mustard and salt. Trim crusts from bread. Spread tuna mixture on 6 slices of bread; cover with remaining bread. Place sandwiches in a buttered baking dish. Top with cheese slices. Combine eggs, milk and Worcestershire sauce; pour over sandwiches. Bake in a 325°F oven 45 minutes, or until a knife inserted in center comes out clean.

Baked New Orleans Fondue

Servings: 6

This dish is a snap to make and you usually have these ingredients on hand.

1 (8 ozs.) can salmon
1 cup minced celery
¼ cup mayonnaise
1 tbs. dry mustard
salt to taste
12 slices bread
6 slices American cheese
3 eggs, beaten
2½ cups milk
2 tsp. Worcestershire sauce

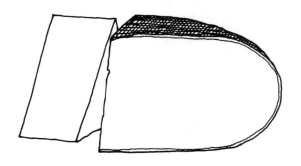

Drain and flake salmon, discarding skin and bones. Combine salmon, celery, mayonnaise, mustard and salt. Trim crusts from bread. Spread salmon mixture on 6 slices of bread and cover with remaining bread. Place sandwiches in a buttered baking dish and top with cheese slices. Combine eggs, milk and Worcestershire sauce and pour over sandwiches. Bake in a 325°F oven 45 minutes, or until a knife inserted in the center comes out clean.

Baked Chicken Fondue

Servings: 4

Serve this with a dry Chenin Blanc or a light red Napa Gamay.

4 egg yolks
4 egg whites, beaten to stiff peaks
1 (10½ ozs.) can cream of chicken soup
1½ cups diced cooked chicken
2-3 tbs. diced pimiento
1 cup grated cheddar cheese
2 cups fresh bread crumbs
salt, cayenne and paprika to taste

Beat egg yolks until light. Add soup, chicken, pimiento, cheese, bread crumbs and seasonings. Fold in stiffly beaten egg whites. Pour into a well-buttered casserole. Bake in a 325°F oven 1 hour, or until a knife inserted in the center comes out clean.

Baked Turkey Fondue
Servings: 4

The green chiles give this dish a little zip. This is a great recipe for the after-Thanksgiving turkey.

1 cup milk
1 cup turkey stock
2 tbs. butter
1¾ cups fresh bread crumbs
2 tbs. lemon juice
1 tsp. thyme

salt and freshly ground pepper to
  taste
⅓ cup canned green chiles, diced
5 egg yolks, beaten
5 egg whites, beaten to stiff peaks
2 cups diced cooked turkey

Heat milk, stock and butter in a heavy saucepan over medium heat. Add bread crumbs, lemon juice, thyme, salt, pepper and green chilies. Stir in beaten egg yolks. Cook, stirring constantly, until thickened. Stir in turkey. Remove from heat and fold in stiffly beaten egg whites. Pour into a well-buttered casserole. Bake in a pan of hot water in a 325°F oven for 1¼ hours, or until a knife inserted in the center comes out clean.

Baked Sausage Fondue

This savory dish is for sausage lovers. Use hot pork sausage if you like spicy things.

1½ lbs. pork sausage
2 tbs. minced green onions
¼ cup chopped pimiento
1 tsp. dry mustard
salt and freshly ground pepper to taste
12 slices bread
6 eggs, beaten
3 cups milk
2 tsp. Worcestershire sauce

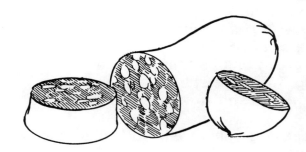

Brown sausage in a frying pan, crumbling into small pieces; drain off fat. Stir in onion, pimiento, mustard, salt and pepper. Trim crusts from bread. Line a buttered baking dish with 6 slices of bread. Cover with sausage mixture and top with remaining bread slices. Combine eggs, milk and Worcestershire sauce; pour over bread. Bake in a 325°F oven for 1½ hours, or until set.

Baked Rice Fondue

Servings: 6

Serve this fondue with an apple walnut salad or stir-fried broccoli.

4 eggs, separated
1½ cups milk
2 cups (8 ozs.) grated sharp cheddar cheese
2 cups cooked rice
3-4 green onions, thinly sliced
2 tsp. Worcestershire
salt and freshly ground pepper to taste

Beat egg yolks well. Add milk, cheese, rice, green onions and seasonings and mix well. Beat egg whites until stiff but not dry. Fold into rice mixture and pour into a buttered casserole. Bake in a pan of hot water in a 350°F oven for 1 hour, or until a knife inserted in the center comes out clean.

Baked Asparagus Fondue

This makes a great accompaniment for a baked ham or pork roast. It is even better when made with fresh, slightly cooked asparagus.

3 slices bread, cubed
1 (10 ozs.) pkg. frozen asparagus, thawed
¾ cup (6 ozs.) grated fontina cheese
1 egg, beaten
1 cup milk
1 tbs. butter, melted
2 tbs. minced onion
2 tsp. Dijon mustard
salt and freshly ground pepper to taste

Arrange layers of bread cubes, asparagus and ½ cup of cheese in a buttered casserole. Blend together egg, milk, butter, onion, mustard, salt and pepper. Pour over casserole ingredients. Sprinkle with remaining cheese. Bake in a 350°F oven 45 minutes, or until a knife inserted in the center comes out clean.

Baked Corn and Cheese Fondue

Servings: 4

Add 1-2 slices of crumbled cooked bacon or ½ cup diced ham to this fondue for a variation.

1 cup milk
1 cup canned corn, drained
1 cup grated cheddar cheese
1½ cups fresh bread crumbs
1 tbs. butter, melted
salt, freshly ground pepper and paprika to taste
3 egg yolks, beaten
3 egg whites, beaten to stiff peaks

Combine milk, corn, cheese, bread crumbs, butter and seasonings. Add beaten egg yolks. Fold in stiffly beaten egg whites. Bake in a well-buttered casserole in a 350°F oven 1 hour, or until a knife inserted in the center comes out clean.

Baked Leek Fondue

Servings: 6

This fondue is delicious as a side dish for grilled salmon or halibut. Serve a dry Riesling wine.

6 slices bread, buttered
1½ cups (6 ozs.) grated Gruyére
  cheese
3 eggs, well beaten
3 cups milk

2 tbs. butter
1 cup diced leeks
¾ tsp. dry mustard
salt and freshly ground pepper to taste

Cut bread into cubes and place in a buttered baking dish. Spread cheese evenly over bread cubes. Melt 2 tbs. butter and sauté leeks for 3 to 4 minutes over low heat until soft. Combine leeks with remaining ingredients and pour over bread. Let stand 2 hours. Bake in a 350°F oven 40 minutes, or until a knife inserted in the center comes out clean.

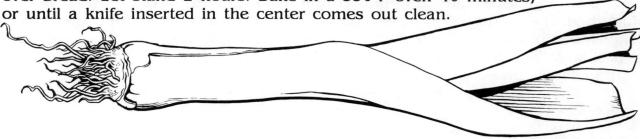

Baked Spinach Fondue

Servings: 4

This pretty green fondue makes a great luncheon dish.

1⅓ cups milk, warmed
1⅓ cups bread crumbs
salt, freshly ground pepper and
  cayenne to taste
1 tsp. Worcestershire sauce
¼ cup melted butter

1/2 cup finely chopped mushrooms
3-4 green onions, thinly sliced
4 eggs, separated
1 cup chopped cooked spinach
⅔ cup grated Gruyére cheese

Combine milk and bread crumbs in top of a double boiler. Let stand 5 minutes. Add salt, pepper, cayenne and Worcestershire. Melt butter in a small skillet. Sauté mushrooms and onions 3 to 4 minutes. Add to bread crumb mixture. Beat egg yolks and blend into crumb mixture. Cook over hot water until thickened. Cool. Add well-drained spinach and cheese to cooled mixture. Beat egg whites to stiff peaks and fold into mixture. Pour into a buttered casserole and bake in a pan of hot water at 350°F for 1 hour, or until a knife inserted in the center comes out clean.

Rarebits

A rarebit as it is prepared today is quite similar to fondue. Originally the bread was toasted, soaked in wine, covered with cheese and toasted again. The result was similar to a grilled sandwich. Today the cheese is melted, as with fondue, and served over toasted bread or English muffin. There is no reason why, if you so desire, you couldn't dip the bread in the rarebit instead. Rarebits are especially nice in the winter for a cozy supper, a brunch or as a snack with crackers for a large crowd.

Quick Welsh Rarebit

Servings: 6-8

This is delicious spooned over cooked broccoli or cauliflower if there is any left over.

1 tbs. butter
2 lbs. American or cheddar cheese, diced
3 tbs. grated onion
2 tsp. Worcestershire sauce
½ tsp. dry mustard
salt, freshly ground pepper and paprika to taste
1 cup ale

Melt butter and cheese in top of a double boiler over hot water, stirring constantly. Add remaining ingredients. Cook, stirring, until mixture is smooth. Serve in a chafing dish or fondue pot with bread cubes for dipping, or spoon over toast.

London Rarebit

Try this with a fontina or Swiss cheese for a variation.

3 tbs. butter
3 tbs. flour
salt to taste
dash Tabasco sauce
½ cup milk
1½ cups (6 ozs.) diced cheddar cheese
¼ cup sherry
1 cup ale

   Melt butter in a saucepan over low heat. Stir in flour and seasonings and let bubble a minute. Remove from heat and slowly add milk. Cook over low heat, stirring constantly, until thickened. Add cheese and sherry, stir until cheese is melted and blend in ale. Serve in a chafing dish or fondue pot with bread cubes for dipping, or spoon over toast.

Spanish Rarebit

Servings: 4

This delicious rarebit makes a wonderful omelet topping.

3 tbs. butter
2 green peppers, chopped
½ cup chopped onion
1 clove garlic, crushed
2 cups (8 ozs.) grated Monterey Jack cheese
1 cup beer
¼ tsp. Tabasco sauce.

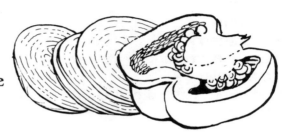

Melt butter in a saucepan or chafing dish. Sauté pepper, onion and garlic for 5 minutes. Slowly add cheese, stirring constantly until melted and smooth. Blend in beer and Tabasco sauce. Serve in a chafing dish or fondue pot with bread cubes for dipping, or spoon over toast.

Sherry Rarebit

Serve this as an appetizer with glasses of dry sherry.

⅓ cup cream
1 lb. Gruyére or fontina cheese, cubed
⅓ cup sherry
½ tsp. Worcestershire sauce
1 tsp. mustard

Combine cream and cheese in top of a double boiler. Cook over hot water until cheese is melted and mixture is smooth. Add Worcestershire sauce and mustard and stir to blend. Serve in a chafing dish or fondue pot with bread cubes for dipping, or spoon over toast.

Rosy Rarebit

Servings: 4

Children love this pretty pink, delicately flavored rarebit.

1 (8 ozs.) can tomatoes
1½ tbs. butter
1 lb. American cheese, diced
salt and freshly ground pepper to taste

Drain tomatoes. Melt butter in a heavy saucepan over low heat. Add drained tomatoes and simmer 20 minutes. Slowly add cheese, stirring constantly until it is melted and mixture has thickened. Season to taste. Serve in a chafing dish or fondue pot with bread cubes for dipping, or spoon over toast.

Cream of Celery Rarebit

Servings: 6

Lightly blanched broccoli or cauliflowerettes, small raw mushrooms and small cooked potatoes make great dippers.

1 (10 ozs.) cream of celery soup
¼ cup dry white wine
½ tsp. mustard
½ tsp. Worcestershire sauce
1½ cups (6 ozs.) diced cheddar cheese
1 egg, well beaten

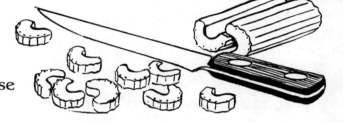

Combine soup, wine, mustard and Worcestershire sauce in a saucepan or chafing dish. Cook over medium heat until mixture is just beginning to boil. Slowly add cheese, stirring constantly until melted. Blend in well beaten egg and continue cooking until mixture reaches desired consistency. Spoon over toast, or serve with bread cubes for dipping.

Eastern Style Rarebit

Servings: 4-6

The sardines add a delicious touch to this rarebit.

Sherry Rarebit, page 83, made with cheddar cheese
1 (4 ozs.) can sardines in oil
1 tbs. butter
salt and freshly ground pepper to taste
8-12 English muffin halves

Prepare rarebit according to directions. Melt butter in a frying pan. Gently sauté sardines about 10 minutes. Using a pancake turner or spatula, lay sautéed sardines on toasted muffin halves. Spoon **Sherry Rarebit** over sardines.

Western Rarebit

This makes a savory Sunday supper dish.

1 (4-5 ozs.) jar dried beef
2 tbs. butter
2 tbs. flour
1½ cups milk
4 ozs. pimiento cheese, diced
2 eggs, beaten
freshly ground pepper to taste

Shred beef and rinse with boiling water; drain well. Melt butter in a heavy saucepan over medium heat. Add flour and blend. Let bubble a minute or two and remove from heat. Slowly stir in milk. Return to heat and cook, stirring until thickened. Add cheese and stir until melted. Mix a little of the hot mixture with the beaten eggs. Stir back into cheese sauce. Add beef and pepper and cook, stirring, until thoroughly heated. Serve over toast.

Spicy Rarebit

If you like hot food, this is for you! Serve with beer or ale.

1 tbs. butter
½ lb. cheddar cheese, diced
½ lb. hot pepper cheese, diced
1 tbs. chili sauce
½ tsp. Tabasco sauce
½ tsp. mustard
salt and freshly ground pepper to taste
6-7 tbs. ale

Melt butter in a heavy saucepan or chafing dish over low heat. Slowly add cheese and stir until melted. Blend in chili sauce, Tabasco, mustard and seasonings. Add ale a tablespoon at a time, stirring. Cook, stirring constantly, until mixture is thickened and smooth. Serve in a chafing dish or fondue pot with bread cubes for dipping or spoon over toast.

Red and Green Rarebit

You can use fresh chopped red and green bell peppers in this dish for a little crunch.

1 lb. American cheese, diced
1 tsp. dry mustard
salt, cayenne and paprika to taste
½ cup ale
2 tbs. chopped canned green chiles
2 tbs. chopped pimiento

Melt cheese in a heavy saucepan over low heat, stirring until smooth. Add mustard, salt, cayenne and paprika. Slowly blend in ale. Add green chiles and pimiento and serve with bread cubes for dipping or spoon over toast.

Frankfurter Rarebit

This quick dish is popular with all ages.

2 tbs. butter
6 frankfurters
2 cups (8 ozs.) shredded American cheese
¾ cup milk
6 slices toast, buttered
1 mild onion, sliced

Melt butter in a frying pan over medium heat. Sauté frankfurters for 15 minutes, until plump and lightly browned. Combine cheese and milk in the top of a double boiler. Cook over hot water, stirring constantly, until cheese melts and mixture is smooth. Slit frankfurters lengthwise, without cutting all the way through. Place, cut sides down, on toast slices. Spoon cheese mixture over franks and garnish with onion slices.

Shrimp Rarebit

Here is a quick appetizer or first course. Serve with a Sauvignon Blanc or Chardonnay.

1 (10 ozs.) cream of mushroom soup
1/2 cup small salad shrimp
1 lb. Monterey Jack cheese, diced
1/4 cup sherry
1/4 tsp. creamed horseradish
2-3 green onions, thinly sliced
salt and freshly ground pepper to taste

Empty soup into the top of a double boiler. Add cheese, place over hot water and stir until cheese is melted. Slowly blend in sherry and seasonings. Cook, stirring, until mixture reaches desired consistency. Add shrimp and heat through. Spoon over toast.

Tuna Rarebit

This makes a delicious supper or winter luncheon dish.

1 tbs. butter
1 tbs. diced cheddar cheese
3 tbs. minced onion
1 tsp. Worcestershire sauce
1 cup ale
½ tsp. dry mustard
salt, freshly ground pepper and paprika to taste
1 (6½ ozs.) can water pack tuna, drained, flaked

Melt butter and cheese together in the top of a double boiler over hot water. Stir constantly until mixture is smooth. Add remaining ingredients and stir until heated and thickened. Serve as a fondue with bread cubes for dipping or spoon over toast.

Dessert Fondue

A dessert fondue is an informal, friendly way to top off a meal. Into these tasty blends of chocolate and other confections, dip chunks of angel food cake, lady fingers, macaroons, plain cookies, pound cake or bite-sized cream puff pastry. Fresh fruits, such as strawberries, grapes, bananas, pears or papayas, make delicious dippers. Dried fruit may also be used. A little bit of care and imagination in arranging your dippers will make any of these dessert fondues a colorful and unusual way to finish a meal. Dessert fondues are also great party fun for children.

Fondue Au Chocolat

Chocolate fondue is actually an American invention. It is said to have originated in a New York restaurant. There are many variations of the basic recipe.

9 ozs. Swiss milk chocolate, broken into pieces
½ cup whipping cream

Combine ingredients in a fondue pot or chafing dish. Stir over very low heat until chocolate is melted and mixture is smooth. Serve with a variety of "dippers."

Variations

- Use bittersweet chocolate instead of milk chocolate.
- Use pretzels of various shapes for dipping.
- Add ½ cup crushed almonds.
- Add 2 tbs. kirsch.
- Add 1 tbs. instant coffee powder.
- Add ¼ tsp. *each* ground cinnamon and ground cloves.
- Add mint flavoring.

Fondue Au Creme

Servings: 4

This simple fondue is rich and delicious, a warm "frosting" for pieces of pound cake, angel food cake, plain cookies or pieces of fresh or dried fruit.

1 cup powdered sugar
1 cup heavy cream
1/2 tsp. flavoring, such as vanilla, almond, mint or lemon extract

Combine sugar and cream in a saucepan. Bring to a boil, stirring constantly. Boil about ½ minute. Pour into a fondue pot or chafing dish. Keep heat as low as possible to prevent scorching. Serve with assorted fruit or cake pieces.

Peanut Butter Fondue

This fondue is for the young crowd and for peanut butter lovers. Bananas are the thing to dip.

4 ozs. peanut butter chips
2 tbs. peanut butter
¾ cup milk
½ tsp. vanilla
2-3 ripe bananas, cut into ¾" chunks

Combine ingredients and melt in fondue pot or in a microwave on medium power. Serve hot.

Chocolate Rum Fondue

This fondue is for chocolate lovers. Strawberries make delicious dippers.

6 ozs. Hershey's Special Dark Chocolate
¼ cup light cream
1 tbs. dark rum

Melt chocolate and cream in a fondue pot or in a microwave on medium power. Stir in rum and serve.

Vanilla Fondue

Servings: 3-4

Dip fresh strawberries or chunks of ripe peaches or pineapple for this dessert.

6 ozs. vanilla milk chips
2 tbs. light cream
1 tbs. Grand Marnier or coffee-flavored liqueur

Melt vanilla chips and cream in a fondue pot or in a microwave on medium power. Stir in liqueur and serve hot.

Butterscotch Fondue

Here is a quick dessert to satisfy a real sweet tooth. If there is any left over, it can be reheated in the microwave and used for an ice cream or dessert sauce.

6 ozs. butterscotch chips
¼ cup evaporated milk
1 tbs. brandy
cubes of pound cake or lady fingers for dipping

Melt butterscotch chips with evaporated milk in a fondue pot over low heat or in a small microwave dish on medium power. Stir in brandy. Serve warm.

Cheddar Cheese Fondue with Apple

Servings: 6

Here is a new twist to that classic combination of apples and cheese, and a refreshing alternative to sweet fondues.

3 tbs. butter
3 tbs. flour
1 cup milk

2 cups (8 ozs.) sharp cheddar cheese, diced
crisp, green apples, cut into chunks

Melt butter in a fondue pot over medium heat. Stir in flour and allow to bubble for 1 minute. Remove from heat and slowly stir in milk. Return to heat and cook, stirring, until mixture thickens and boils. Add diced cheese and stir until melted and smooth. Serve with green apples.

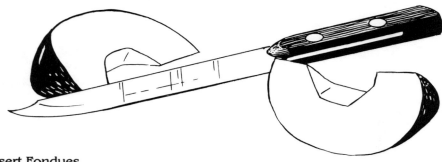

Index

NOTES

NOTES

NOTES

METRIC CONVERSION CHART

Liquid or Dry Measuring Cup
(based on an 8 ounce cup)
1/4 cup = 60 ml
1/3 cup = 80 ml
1/2 cup = 125 ml
3/4 cup = 190 ml
1 cup = 250 ml
2 cups = 500 ml

Liquid or Dry Measuring Cup
(based on a 10 ounce cup)
1/4 cup = 80 ml
1/3 cup = 100 ml
1/2 cup = 150 ml
3/4 cup = 230 ml
1 cup = 300 ml
2 cups = 600 ml

Liquid or Dry
Teaspoon and Tablespoon
1/4 tsp. = 1.5 ml
1/2 tsp. = 3 ml
1 tsp. = 5 ml
3 tsp. = 1 tbs. = 15 ml

Temperatures

°F		°C
200	=	100
250	=	120
275	=	140
300	=	150
325	=	160
350	=	180
375	=	190
400	=	200
425	=	220
450	=	230
475	=	240
500	=	260
550	=	280

Pan Sizes (1 inch = 25mm)
8-inch pan (round or square) = 200 mm x 200 mm
9-inch pan (round or square) = 225 mm x 225 mm
9 x 5 x 3-inch loaf pan = 225 mm x 125 mm x 75 mm
1/4 inch thickness = 5 mm
1/8 inch thickness = 2.5 mm

Pressure Cooker
100 Kpa = 15 pounds per square inch
70 Kpa = 10 pounds per square inch
35 Kpa = 5 pounds per square inch

Mass
1 ounce = 30 g
4 ounces = 1/4 pound = 125 g
8 ounces = 1/2 pounds = 250 g
16 ounces = 1 pound = 500 g
2 pounds = 1 kg

Key   (America uses an 8 ounce cup — Britain uses a 10 ounce cup)

ml = milliliter
l = liter
g = gram
K = Kilo (one thousand)
mm = millimeter
m = mill (a thousandth)
°F = degrees Fahrenheit

°C = degrees Celsius
tsp. = teaspoon
tbs. = tablespoon
Kpa = (pounds pressure per square inch)
     This configuration is used for pressure
     cookers only.

Metric equivalents are rounded to conform to existing metric measuring utensils.

Serve Creative, Easy, Nutritious Meals with nitty gritty® Cookbooks

100 Dynamite Desserts
The 9 x 13 Pan Cookbook
The Barbecue Cookbook *(new)*
Beer and Good Food
The Best Bagels are Made at Home
The Best Pizza is Made at Home*(new)*
Bread Baking
Bread Machine Cookbook
Bread Machine Cookbook II
Bread Machine Cookbook III
Bread Machine Cookbook IV
Bread Machine Cookbook V
Bread Machine Cookbook VI
Cappuccino/Espresso
Casseroles *(new)*
The Coffee Book
Convection Oven Cookery *(new)*
Cooking for 1 or 2
Cooking in Clay
Cooking in Porcelain
Cooking with Chile Peppers
Cooking with Grains
Cooking with Your Kids
Creative Mexican Cooking
Deep Fried Indulgences

The Dehydrator Cookbook
Easy Vegetarian Cooking
Edible Pockets for Every Meal
Entrées From Your Bread Machine
Extra-Special Crockery Pot Recipes
Fabulous Fiber Cookery
Fondue and Hot Dips
Fresh Vegetables
From Freezer, 'Fridge and Pantry
From Your Ice Cream Maker
The Garlic Cookbook
Gourmet Gifts
Healthy Cooking on the Run
Healthy Snacks for Kids
Indoor Grilling
The Juicer Book
The Juicer Book II
Lowfat American Favorites
Marinades
Muffins, Nut Breads and More
The New Blender Book
New International Fondue Cookbook
No Salt, No Sugar, No Fat
One-Dish Meals
Oven and Rotisserie Roasting

Party Fare
The Pasta Machine Cookbook
Pinch of Time: Meals in Less than 30
    Minutes
Quick and Easy Pasta Recipes
Recipes for the Loaf Pan
Recipes for the Pressure Cooker
Recipes for Yogurt Cheese
Risottos, Paellas, and other Rice
    Specialties
The Sandwich Maker Cookbook
The Sensational Skillet: Sautés and
    Stir-Fries *(new)*
Slow Cooking in Crock-Pot,® Slow
    Cooker, Oven and Multi-Cooker
The Steamer Cookbook
The Toaster Oven Cookbook
Unbeatable Chicken Recipes
The Versatile Rice Cooker
Waffles
The Well Dressed Potato
The Wok
Worldwide Sourdoughs from Your
    Bread Machine
Wraps and Roll-Ups

For a free catalog, call: Bristol Publishing Enterprises, Inc.
(800) 346-4889
www.bristolcookbooks.com